C...

Sarah Kane

'It is a poetic, musical quartet for four voices, of great formal beauty, with echoes of the Bible, the Book of Common Prayer and T S Eliot' *Daily Telegraph*

'An oddly beautiful chamber quartet for inflamed yet bewildered souls' *The Times*

'Four nameless characters from an unidentifiable city, tell their tales of disintegration and isolation. Their dialogues meet, converge and move apart with balletic grace, with caustically humorous as well as distressing consequences. Kane uses the inherent schizophrenia of such a style brilliantly . . .' *Time Out*

Sarah Kane was born in 1971. Her first play *Blasted* was produced at the Royal Court Theatre Upstairs in 1995. Her second play, *Phaedra's Love*, was produced at the Gate Theatre in 1996. In April 1998, *Cleansed* was produced at the Royal Court Theatre Downstairs and in September 1998, *Crave* was produced by Paines Plough and Bright Ltd at the Traverse Theatre, Edinburgh. Her last play, *4.48 Psychosis*, premiered at the Royal Court Jerwood Theatre Upstairs in June 2000. Her short film *Skin*, produced by British Screen/Channel Four, premiered in June 1997. Sarah Kane died in 1999.

KA 0272937 7

Published by Methuen 2002

1 3 5 7 9 10 8 6 4 2

This edition first published in Great Britain in 2002 by
Methuen Publishing Ltd, 215 Vauxhall Bridge Road, London SW1V 1EJ

Crave first published in 1998 by Methuen,
copyright © 1998 Sarah Kane

Sarah Kane has asserted her rights under the Copyright, Designs and Patents
Act, 1988, to be identified as the author of this work.

Methuen Publishing Limited Reg. No. 3543167

A CIP catalogue record for this book
is available from the British Library

ISBN 0 413 72880 3

Typeset by Deltatype Ltd, Birkenhead
Printed and bound in Great Britain by
Cox and Wyman Ltd, Reading, Berkshire

Caution

All rights in this play are strictly reserved and application for performance etc.
should be made to: Casarotto Ramsay & Associates Ltd, National House,
60–66 Wardour Street, London W1V 4ND. No performance may be given
unless a licence has been obtained.

This book is sold subject to the condition that it shall not,
by way of trade or otherwise, be lent, resold, hired out, or otherwise
circulated in any form of binding or cover other than that in which it
is published and without a similar condition being imposed on
the subsequent purchaser.

KING ALFRED'S COLLEGE
WINCHESTER

02729347 822.91
KAN

Crave

My thanks to Vicky Featherstone, Alan Westaway, Catherine Cusack, Andrew Maud, Kathryn Howdon, Mel Kenyon, Nils Tabert, Domingo Ledezma, Jelena Pejíc, Elana Greenfield and New Dramatists.

For Mark.

Crave was premiered by Paines Plough at the Traverse Theatre, Edinburgh on 13 August 1998. The cast was as follows:

C Sharon Duncan-Brewster
M Ingrid Craigie
B Paul Thomas Hickey
A Alan Williams

Director   Vicky Featherstone
Designer   Georgia Sion
Lighting by   Nigel J. Edwards

Characters

C
M
B
A

Author's note

Punctuation is used to indicate delivery, not to conform to the rules of grammar.

A stroke (/) indicates the point of interruption in overlapping dialogue.

Editor's note

This edition of *Crave*, first reprinted in 2000, incorporates minor revisions made to the original text by Sarah Kane shortly before her death. It should therefore be regarded as the definitive version in all respects.

C You're dead to me.

B My will reads, Fuck this up and I'll haunt you for the rest of your fucking life.

C He's following me.

A What do you want?

B To die.

C Somewhere outside the city, I told my mother, You're dead to me.

B No that's not it.

C If I could be free of you without having to lose you.

A Sometimes that's not possible.

M I keep telling people I'm pregnant. They say How did you do it, what are you taking? I say I drank a bottle of port, smoked some fags and fucked a stranger.

B All lies.

C He needs to have a secret but he can't help telling. He thinks we don't know. Believe me, we know.

M A voice in the desert.

C He who comes after.

M There is something in the way.

A Still here.

C Three summers ago I was bereaved. No one died but I lost my mother.

A She had him back.

C I believe in anniversaries. That a mood can be repeated even if the event that caused it is trivial or forgotten. In this case it's neither.

M I will grow older and I will, it will, something

B I smoke till I'm sick.

A   Black on white and blue.

C   When I wake I think my period must have started or rather never stopped because it only finished three days ago.

M   The heat is going out of me.

C   The heart is going out of me.

B   I feel nothing, nothing.
I feel nothing.

M   Is it possible?

B   Sorry?

A   I'm not a rapist.

M   David?

   A beat.

B   Yeah.

A   I'm a paedophile.

M   Do you remember me?

   A beat.

B   Yeah.

C   Looks like a German,

A   Talks like a Spaniard,

C   Smokes like a Serb.

M   You've forgotten.

C   All things to all men.

B   I don't think

M   Yes.

C   I couldn't forget.

M   I looked for you. All over the city.

B   I really don't

M Yes. Yes.

A You do.

M Yes.

C Please stop this.

M And now I have found you.

C Someone has died who is not dead.

A And now we are friends.

C It's not my fault, it was never my fault.

M Everything that happens is supposed to happen.

B Where you been?

M Here and there.

C Leave.

B Where?

C Now.

M There.

A Because love by its nature desires a future.

C If she'd left –

M I want a child.

B I can't help you.

C None of this would have happened.

M Time is passing and I don't have time.

C None of it.

B No.

C None.

A In a lay-by on the motorway going out of the city, or maybe in, depending on which way you look, a small dark girl sits in the passenger seat of a parked car. Her elderly grandfather undoes his trousers and it pops out of his pants, big and purple.

C I feel nothing, nothing.
I feel nothing.

A And when she cries, her father in the back seat says I'm sorry, she's not normally like this.

M Haven't we been here before?

A And though she cannot remember she cannot forget.

C And has been hurtling away from that moment ever since.

B Will you come round and seduce me? I need to be seduced by an older woman.

M I'm not an older woman.

B Older than me, not older *per se*.

C You've fallen in love with someone that doesn't exist.

A Tragedy.

B Really.

M Oh yes.

A What do you want?

C To die.

B To sleep.

M No more.

A And the bus driver loses it, stops the bus in the middle of the road, climbs out of his cab, strips off his clothes and walks down the street, his cute little arse shining in the sun.

B I drink till I'm sick.

C Everywhere I go, I see him. I know the plates, I know the car, does he think I don't know?

A You're never as powerful as when you know you're powerless.

B I shake when I don't have it.

M Bleeding.

B Brain melts when I do.

M I ran through the poppy field at the back of my grandfather's farm. When I burst in through the kitchen door I saw him sitting with my grandmother on his lap. He kissed her on the lips and caressed her breast. They looked around and saw me, smiling at my confusion. When I related this to my mother more than ten years later she stared at me oddly and said 'That didn't happen to you. It happened to me. My father died before you were born. When that happened I was pregnant with you, but I didn't know it until the day of his funeral.'

C We pass these messages.

M Someone somewhere is crying for me, crying for my death.

B My fingers inside her, my tongue in her mouth.

C I wish to live with myself.

A No witnesses.

M And if this makes no sense then you understand perfectly.

A It's not what you think.

C No that's not it.

M Time after time, same fucking excuse.

C LEAVE.

A COME BACK.

All STAY.

C Can't have this again.

A Stunned.

B   Stoned.

M   I have a black black side I know. I have a side so green you will never know.

B   Have another drink, another cigarette.

M   Sometimes the shape of my head alarms me. When I catch sight of it reflected in a darkened train window, the landscape passing through the image of my head. Not that there is anything unusual or . . . alarming . . . about the shape of my head, but it does . . . alarm me.

A   Why do you do this?

C   I find it alarming.

M   There's so little time.

C   I hate the smell of my own family.

B   Base 1.
Base 2.
Base 3.
Bingo.

C   You'll smell better when you're dead than you do now.

A   An American woman translated a novel from Spanish into English. She asked her Spanish classmate his opinion of her work. The translation was very bad. He said he would help her and she offered to pay him for his time. He refused. She offered to take him out to dinner. This was acceptable to him so he agreed. But she forgot. The Spaniard is still waiting for his dinner.

B   El dinero viene solo.

C   Alone.

M   If love would come.

B   It's just not me.

A   Has it ever occurred to you you're looking in the wrong place?

M Now.

B Never.

C No.

B It's very nice. Will you make me one?

M It's made of egg shells and concrete.

B Will you make me one?

M Concrete, paint and egg shells.

B I didn't ask what it was made of, I asked if you'd make me one.

M Every time I have an egg I stick the shell on there and spray it.

C She sees through walls.

B Will. You. Make. Me. One.

C Other lives.

A A mother beats her child savagely because it runs out in front of a car.

M You stop thinking of yourself as I, you think of we.

B Let's just go to/bed.

C no no no no no no no no no

A A wish under pressure.

C Cry blue murder.

M Do not remove your gloves until you leave the last town.

B Are you a lesbian?

M Oh please.

B I thought that might be why you don't have children.

A Why?

M I never met a man I trusted.

C   Why what?

B   You trust me?

M   This has nothing to do with you.

C   Why what?

M   I'm not interested in you.

C   Why what, why what?

M   I'm not interested in the first fucking thing about you.

A   I don't drink. I hate smoking. I'm vegetarian. I don't fuck around. I've never visited a prostitute and I've never had a sexually transmitted disease other than thrush. This does, I'm afraid, make me a rarity, if not unique.

B   Look.

C   Listen.

B   Look. My nose.

M   What about it.

B   What do you think?

C   Broken.

B   I've never broken a bone in my body.

A   Like Christ.

B   But my Dad has. Smashed his nose in a car crash when he was eighteen. And I've got this. Genetically impossible, but there it is. We pass these messages faster than we think and in ways we don't think possible.

C   If I was
         If I
         If I was

M   HURRY UP PLEASE IT'S TIME – go to seats

B   And don't you think that a child conceived by rape would suffer?

C But as it is.

M You think I'm going to rape you? *— walking behind*

C Yes.

A No.

B Yes.

M No. *stand up*

A No.

B Yes.

C Yes.

M Is that possible?

C I see no good in anyone any more.

B Okay, I was, okay, I was, okay okay. I was, okay, two people, right?

A Okay.

B One of these days,

C Soon very soon,

M Now. *acting out*

A But looks aren't everything.

B It's just not me.

A A small boy had an imaginary friend. He took her to the beach and they played in the sea. A man came from the water and took her away. The following morning the body of a girl was found washed up on the beach.

M What's that got to do with anything?

A Clutching a fistful of sand.

B Everything.

C What's anything got to do with anything?

M   Nothing.

A   Exactly.

B   That's the worst of it.

M   Nothing.

C   Is this what it is?
Is this it?

M   How much longer

B   How many more times

A   How much more

C   Corrupt or inept.

B   I am nobody's windfall.

A   I'm sorry.

C   Go away.

M   Now.

C   Go away.

B   I'm sorry.

C   Go away.

A   I'm sorry, I'm sorry, I'm sorry, I'm sorry, I'm sorry,
I'm sorry, I'm sorry.

C   What for?

M   Have you ever raped anyone?

A   I'm sorry I'm following you.

B   No.

M   Why not?

A   There're worse things than being fat and fifty.

M   Why not?

A   Being dead and thirty.

M I'm the kind of woman about whom people say Who *was* that woman?

A The question is Where do you live and where do you want to live?

M Absence sleeps between the buildings at night.

C Don't die.

B This city, fucking love it, wouldn't live nowhere else, couldn't.

M Where do you find it?

C Where do I start?

A A Japanese man in love with his virtual reality girlfriend.

B You look reasonably happy for someone who's not.

M Where do I stop?

A Swords in turmoil.

B Here.

C I'm looking for a time and place free of things that crawl, fly or sting.

M Inside.

A Here.

M Be the one.

C If she'd left –

M I don't want to grow old and cold and be too poor to dye my hair.

C You get mixed messages because I have mixed feelings.

M I don't want to be living in a bedsit at sixty, too scared to turn the heater on because I can't pay the bill.

C What ties me to you is guilt.

M I don't want to die alone and not be found till my bones are clean and the rent overdue.

C   I don't want to stay.

B   I don't want to stay.

C   I want you to leave.

M   If love would come.

A   Let it happen.

C   No.

M   It's leaving me behind.

B   No.

C   No.

M   Yes.

B   No.

A   Yes.

C   No.

M   Yes.

B   Let me go.

C   I don't want to have to buy you Christmas presents any more.

B   Just a name would be nice.

M   You're very naïve if you think you still have those kind of choices.

B   My back aches.

C   My head aches.

A   My heart aches.

M   You shouldn't sleep next to the radiator.

B   Where should I sleep?

M   Do you want a massage?

C   Don't touch me.

M I shouldn't be doing this.

A One touch.

B Will you get into trouble?

A An isolated act.

M No, I . . . mustn't get attached.

A It's only natural.

B Seeing another human being in distress.

C I feel
I just feel

M You asked me to seduce you.

B Not tie me up.

A Be grateful.

C As a child I liked to piss on the carpet.
The carpet rotted and I blamed it on the dog.

M I'm unable to know you.

C Don't want to know me.

M Utterly unknowable.

A Still here.

M I need a child.

B That's all?

C It's everything.

M That's all.

B Meni ni iz džepa, ni u džep.

C Mother.

A The king is dead, long live the king.

B If it could be an act of love.

C I can't remember

B   Whose

C   Any more

A   Why do you think that is?

C   My mind's a blank.

M   Why are you laughing?

C   Someone has died.

B   You think I'm laughing?

M   Why are you crying?

C   You're dead to me.

B   You think I'm crying?

C   I'll cry if you laugh.

B   You could be my mother.

M   I'm not your mother.

A   Baby.

M   now now now now now now now

C   Am I an unnecessary complication?

B   A sporadic addict.

A   No one but you.

B   Addicted to sickness.

A   It's not you, it's me.

C   It's always me.

A   I want to sleep next to you and do your shopping and carry your bags and tell you how much I love being with you but they keep making me do stupid things.

M   It's not me, it's you.

B   Pointless fucking

M   Time sheet.

C   Six month plan.

A   And I want to play hide-and-seek and give you my
clothes and tell you I like your shoes and sit on the steps
while you take a bath and massage your neck and kiss
your feet and hold your hand and go for a meal and not
mind when you eat my food and meet you at Rudy's and
talk about the day and type up your letters and carry your
boxes and laugh at your paranoia and give you tapes you
don't listen to and watch great films and watch terrible
films and complain about the radio and take pictures of
you when you're sleeping and get up to fetch you coffee
and bagels and Danish and go to Florent and drink coffee
at midnight and have you steal my cigarettes and never
be able to find a match and tell you about the tv
programme I saw the night before and take you to the
eye hospital and not laugh at your jokes and want you in
the morning but let you sleep for a while and kiss your
back and stroke your skin and tell you how much I love
your hair your eyes your lips your neck your breasts your
arse your

and sit on the steps smoking till your neighbour comes
home and sit on the steps smoking till *you* come home
and worry when you're late and be amazed when you're
early and give you sunflowers and go to your party and
dance till I'm black and be sorry when I'm wrong and
happy when you forgive me and look at your photos and
wish I'd known you forever and hear your voice in my
ear and feel your skin on my skin and get scared when
you're angry and your eye has gone red and the other
eye blue and your hair to the left and your face oriental
and tell you you're gorgeous and hug you when you're
anxious and hold you when you hurt and want you when
I smell you and offend you when I touch you and
whimper when I'm next to you and whimper when I'm
not and dribble on your breast and smother you in the
night and get cold when you take the blanket and hot
when you don't and melt when you smile and dissolve
when you laugh and not understand why you think I'm

rejecting you when I'm not rejecting you and wonder
how you could think I'd ever reject you and wonder who
you are but accept you anyway and tell you about the
tree angel enchanted forest boy who flew across the
ocean because he loved you and write poems for you and
wonder why you don't believe me and have a feeling so
deep I can't find words for it and want to buy you a
kitten I'd get jealous of because it would get more
attention than me and keep you in bed when you have to
go and cry like a baby when you finally do and get rid of
the roaches and buy you presents you don't want and
take them away again and ask you to marry me and you
say no *again* but keep on asking because though you think
I don't mean it I do always have from the first time I
asked you and wander the city thinking it's empty
without you and want what you want and think I'm
losing myself but know I'm safe with you and tell you the
worst of me and try to give you the best of me because
you don't deserve any less and answer your questions
when I'd rather not and tell you the truth when I really
don't want to and try to be honest because I know you
prefer it and think it's all over but hang on in for just ten
more minutes before you throw me out of your life and
forget who I am and try to get closer to you because it's
beautiful learning to know you and well worth the effort
and speak German to you badly and Hebrew to you
worse and make love with you at three in the morning
and somehow somehow somehow communicate
some of the/overwhelming undying overpowering
unconditional all-encompassing heart-enriching
mind-expanding on-going never-ending love I have
for you.

C   (*Under her breath until* **A** *stops speaking.*) this has to stop this
has to stop this has to stop this has to stop this has to stop
this has to stop this has to stop this has to stop (*Then at
normal volume.*) this has to stop this has to stop this has
to stop

A   Don't they *understand?* I've got *important* things to do.

C   It's getting worse.

A   I am lost, so fucking lost in this mess of a woman.

B   She wants a kid yesterday.

A   What will I do when you throw me away?

C   Listen.

B   Look.

C   Listen. I am here to remember. I need to . . . remember.
       I have this grief and I don't know why.

A   You're always gorgeous, but you're particularly gorgeous
       when you come.

C   That violent terrified paralysed child.

A   As she gets more and more angry off come more and more
       clothes as it gets less and less likely she'll let me
       anywhere near her.

B   I have a bad bad feeling about this bad bad feeling.

A   I am so lonely, so fucking lonely.

C   I didn't

A   I don't

C   Understand

M   Control, control, relax and control.

A   It is this woman with the desolate eyes for whom I would
       die.

C   Her hair is white, but for some reason – perhaps because
       her hair is white – I have no idea how old she is.

M   Sunny landscapes. Pastel walls. Gentle air conditioning.

A   I keep trying to understand but I don't.

C   I look at the large beige hessian cushion, try to connect, try
       to decipher myself woven into the clean blank fabric.

A When does it stop?

C And then at the paisley green cushion, a thoroughly inappropriate cushion to represent any part of me, especially the parts I am showing to her.

M Do you have difficulty in relationships with men?

A busy happy busy happy busy happy

M Do you *have* relationships with men?

B The only thing I want to say I've said already, and it's a bit fucking tedious to say it again, no matter how true it is, no matter that it's the one unifying thought humanity has.

A HOW CAN YOU LEAVE ME LIKE THIS?

C My grief has nothing to do with men. I'm having a breakdown because I'm going to die.

A Long before I had the chance to adore all of you, I adored the bits of you I could see.

B The woman with dragon eyes.

A Blue into green.

C All blue.

A I don't have music, Christ I wish I had music but all I have is words.

B Du bist die Liebe meines Lebens.

A Don't cut me out.

B Something inside me that kicks like a bastard.

C A dull ache in my solar plexus.

B Gag for a fag.

M Have you ever been hospitalised?

A Pain by association.

C I need a miracle to save me.

M What for?

A Insanity.

C Anorexia. Bulimia.

B Whatever.

C No.

M Never.

C Sorry.

A The truth is simple.

C I'm evil, I'm damaged, and no one can save me.

A Death is an option.

B I disgust myself.

C Depression's inadequate. A full scale emotional collapse is the minimum required to justify letting everyone down.

A The coward's way out,

C I don't have the courage.

B I think about you

A Dream about you

B Talk about you

A Can't get you out of my system.

M It's okay.

B I like you in my system.

M No performance needed.

C One fine morning in the month of May.

B No that's not it.

C You could be my mother.

M I'm not your mother.

C   I have this guilt and I don't know why.

A   Only love can save me and love has destroyed me.

C   A field. A basement. A bed. A car.

B   In a day or two I'll go back for another affair, although the affair is now so on-going it almost constitutes a relationship.

M   Go on.

B   If you don't want me to come I won't come. You can say, it doesn't matter. I mean it matters but it's better to say. Then I'll know. So.

M   Beyond the pale.

A   Beyond the pain.

M   Choose, focus, apply.

B   I fancy my chances.

C   I buy a new tape recorder and blank tapes.

B   I always do.

C   I have old ones that will do just as well in actuality, but the truth has little to do with actuality, and the point (if there is one) is to record the truth.

A   I am so tired.

C   I crave white on white and black, but my thoughts race in glorious technicolour, prodding me awake, whipping away the warm blanket of invisibility every time it swears to smother my mind in nothing.

A   Most people,

B   They get on,

A   They get up,

B   They get on.

A   My hollow heart is full of darkness.

C   One touch record.

M   Filled with emptiness.

B   Satisfied with nothing.

A   One touch.

M   Record.

C   My bowel curls at his touch.

A   Poor, poor love.

C   I feel nothing, nothing.
I feel nothing.

B   I came back.

C   If she'd left –

A   I'm going to die.

M   This abuse has gone on long enough.

C   Maggots everywhere.

B   There's no one like you.

C   Whenever I look really close at something, it swarms with white larvae.

A   Black folding in.

C   I open my mouth and I too am full of them, crawling down my throat.

B   Something happened.

A   So aghast.

C   I try to pull it out but it gets longer and longer, there's no end to it. I swallow it and pretend it isn't there.

B   Imperceptibly slowly and in an instant.

A   Nothing spectacular.

B   I keep coming back.

A A horror so deep only ritual can contain it,

M Express it,

B Explain it,

A Maintain it.

B Besos brujos que me matan.

C The navy denim dress I wore at six, the elastic red and blue belt tight round my waist, nylon socks, the hard crust of scabs on my knees, the metal barred climbing frame between my legs, David –

A NO.

M I cannot love you because I cannot respect you.

C Clean slate, long love.

M I was catching a plane. A psychic predicted that I would not get on this flight but that my lover would. The plane would crash and he would be killed. I didn't know what to do. If I missed the flight I would be fulfilling the prophecy so risking my lover's death. But in order to break the prophecy I would have to get on a plane which seemed destined to crash.

A What did you do?

M Begin again.

A Begin again.

C Purple heather scratching my legs.

A Anything but this.

C A handsome blond fourteen year old, his thumbs hooked over his jeans half exposing his buttocks, his blue blue eyes full of the sun.

B Sick of it, man, I'm totally fucking sick of it.

A What did you do?

B Nothing, nothing, I did nothing.

M None of this matters because I'm simply not in love with you.

A And I am shaking, sobbing with the memory of her, when she loved me, before I was her torturer, before there was no room in me for her, before we misunderstood, in fact the very first moment I saw her, her eyes smiling and full of the sun, and I shudder with grief for that moment which I've been hurtling away from ever since.

B Begin again, begin again.

M Move on.

A I look at her breast,

C A balloon of milk,

M Sooner or later,

C A bubble of blood,

B One way or another,

C Gurgling blood,

B That is going into my mouth,

C Thick yellow blood,

A My pain is nothing compared to hers.

C but but but

A (and this is crucial)

B Don't say no to me.

C I keep coming back.

B You have this effect.

M You can't say no.

A Dark angel divine.

C It's not him I want.

A I fucking miss you.

C It's my virginity.

B I miss fucking you.

C A fourteen year old to steal my virginity on the moor and rape me till I come.

M One of these days

B Soon very soon

A Love you till then

M (and after?)

C I have children, the men come, I am fighting but they take them, I realise, the men, they came, they said, in the night, they said

A don't say no to me you can't say no to me because it's such a relief to have love again and to lie in bed and be held and touched and kissed and adored and your heart will leap when you hear my voice and see my smile and feel my breath on your neck and your heart will race when I want to see you and I will lie to you from day one and use you and screw you and break your heart because you broke mine first and you will love me more each day until the weight is unbearable and your life is mine and you'll die alone because I will take what I want then walk away and owe you nothing it's always there it's always been there and you cannot deny the life you feel fuck that life fuck that life fuck that life I have lost you now

C GOT ME

B Now I have found you I can stop looking for myself.

C She touched my arm and smiled.

B One of those faces I could never have imagined.

A We checked into a hotel pretending we weren't going to have sex.

C Eyes, whispers, shades and shadows.

M Where you going who you seeing what you doing?

B Jebem radoznale.

A I have to be where I want to be.

M Can't have this again.

A We made love, then she threw up.

C No one to help me not my fucking mother neither.

A I crossed two rivers and wept by one.

M I close my eyes and I see her close her eyes and she sees you.

A The scream of a daffodil,

M The stain of a scream.

C I watched my father beat my mother with a walking stick.

A A stain,

C An echo,

A A stain.

B I'm sorry you saw that.

C I'm sorry he did it.

A I despair of despair.

M No regrets.

A I swear I can't bear to look at you.

C I did nothing, nothing.

B I did nothing.

C I want to feel physically like I feel emotionally.
Starved.

M Beaten.

A Broken.

C   He buys me a make-up kit, blushers and lipstick and eyeshadow. And I paint my face in bruises and blood and cuts and swelling, and on the mirror in deep red, UGLY.

A   Death is my lover and he wants to move in.

B   What does that mean, what does that mean, what does that mean what you're saying?

C   Be a woman, be a woman, FUCK YOU.

M   There's something very unflattering about being desired when the other person is so drunk they can't see.

B   Fuck you.

C   I tried to explain that I don't want to sleep with someone who won't appreciate how hard it was for me the following morning, but he'd passed out by the time I finished my sentence.

M   QED.

C   Still sleeping with Daddy.

A   The games we play,

M   The lies we tell.

B   Your hair is an act of God.

A   A Vietnamese girl, her entire existence given meaning and permanence in the thirty seconds she fled from her village, skin melting, mouth open.

C   No one can hate me more than I hate myself.

A   I am not what I am, I am what I do.

M   This is terrible.

C   This is true.

A   The thing I swore I'd never do, the thing I swore I'd –

M   All that pain

C   Forever

B   Till now.

A On my children's lives, my children's love.

M Why do you drink so much?

B The fags aren't killing me fast enough.

C My laughter is a bubble of despair.

M Rule one.

C No records.

M No letters.

A No credit card bills for afternoons in hotel rooms, no receipts for expensive jewellery, no calling at home then hanging up in silence.

C No feeling,

B No emotion,

M A cold fuck and a goldfish memory.

C My bowels gave way.

A Throbbing between shame and guilt.

C Mess. Mess.

A She knows.

B It's just not me.

A Never keep souvenirs of a murder.

M Everything's clear.

C Another girl,

B Another life.

C I did nothing, nothing.

B I did nothing.

M Beyond the pale.

A God forgive me I want to be clean.

C He screams at me to see what I have become.

M Go on.

C Why can no one make love to me the way I want to be loved?

M I could be your mother.

B You're not my mother.

M Soon very soon.

B Now.

C I've faked orgasms before, but this is the first time I've faked *not* having an orgasm.

A From under the door seeps a black pool of blood.

M Why?

C What?

B Why what?

A What?

M When he's generous, kind, thoughtful and happy, I know he's having an affair.

C He thinks we're stupid, he thinks we don't know.

M A third person in my bed whose face eludes me.

B Just me,

A Just the way I am,

C Nothing to be done.

M Give, sympathise, control.

B Now.

C So tired of secrets.

M It's just not me.

C She is currently having some kind of nervous breakdown and wishes she'd been born black, male and more attractive.

B   I give myself.

C   Or just more attractive.

B   I give my heart.

C   Or just different.

M   But that's not really giving.

C   Just someone fucking else.

A   Fragile and choking.

C   She ceases to continue with the day to day farce of getting through the next few hours in an attempt to ward off the fact that she doesn't know how to get through the next forty years.

A   I love you still,

B   Against my will.

C   She's talking about herself in the third person because the idea of being who she is, of acknowledging that she is herself, is more than her pride can take.

B   With a fucking vengeance.

C   She's sick to the fucking gills of herself and wishes wishes wishes that something would happen to make life begin.

A   I'm a much nicer person since I had an affair.

C   You can only kill yourself if you're not already dead.

M   Guilt does that.

A   Because now I know that betrayal means nothing.

C   Two women at the foot of a cross.

B   A flower opens in the heat of the sun.

A   A face screaming into hollow nothing.

B   It's real, it's real, dead real, dead real.

M   A private iconography which I cannot decipher,

A   Beyond my comprehension,

C   Beyond my

A   Beyond

B   There's a difference between articulacy and intelligence. I can't articulate the difference but there is one.

M   Empty.

A   Sickened.

C   White.

B   Love me.

A   Guilt lingers like the smell of death and nothing can free me from this cloud of blood.

C   You killed my mother.

A   She was already dead.

M   If you want me to abuse you I will abuse you.

A   She died.

B   People die.

M   It happens.

C   My entire life is waiting to see the person with whom I am currently obsessed, starving the weeks away until our next fifteen minute appointment.

A   MNO

C   I write the truth and it kills me.

B   On the run.

M   Nowhere to hide.

C   I hate these words that keep me alive
      I hate these words that won't let me die

B   Expressing my pain without easing it.

C   Ha ha ha

B   Ho ho ho

M   He he he

C   It is not acceptable for me to be me.

A   You're losing your mind in front of my eyes.

M   It slipped silently out of control.

B   Let me.

M   Go.

A   A small girl became increasingly paralysed by her parents' frequently violent rows. Sometimes she would spend hours standing completely still in the toilet, simply because that was where she happened to be when the fight began. Finally, in moments of calm, she would take bottles of milk from the fridge or doorstep and leave them in places where she may later become trapped. Her parents were unable to understand why they found bottles of sour milk in every room in the house.

M   Why?

C   What?

B   Why what?

C   What?

M   Why are you crying?

A   There's no news here.

B   You were so persistent.

C   It's always me.

M   You always knew this.

B   It's out of control.

C   How did I lose you?

A   You threw me away.

C   No.

M Yes.

B No.

A Yes.

B No.

C No.

A Yes.

   A beat.

B No.

C No.

M Yes.

B No.

C No.

A Yes.

C No.

   A beat.

A Yes.

C No.

B No.

M Yes.

A Yes.

M Yes.

C (*Emits a short one syllable scream.*)

   A beat.

C (*Emits a short one syllable scream.*)

B (*Emits a short one syllable scream.*)

M (*Emits a short one syllable scream.*)

B   (*Emits a short one syllable scream.*)

A   (*Emits a short one syllable scream.*)

M   (*Emits a short one syllable scream.*)

C   (*Emits a short one syllable scream.*)

   A beat.

M   If you won't talk, I can't help you.

B   This place.

C   ES3.

A   I am the beast at the end of the rope.

C   Silence or violence.

B   The choice is yours.

C   Don't fill my stomach if you can't fill my heart.

B   You fill my head as only someone who is absent can.

M   Impaired judgement, sexual dysfunction, anxiety, headaches, nervousness, sleeplessness, restlessness, nausea, diarrhoea, itching, shaking, sweating, twitching.

C   That's what I'm suffering from *now*.

M   It's okay.

B   It won't matter.

A   It doesn't matter.

C   Put me down or put me away.

A   No one survives life.

C   And no one can know what the night is like.

M   Has it ever occurred to you you're in the wrong place?

C   No.

B   Never.

A   No.

C   If I die here I was murdered by daytime television.

A   I lied for you and that is why I cannot love you.

M   Do not demand,

A   Do not entreat,

B   Learn, learn, why can't I learn?

C   They switch on my light every hour to check I'm still breathing.

B   Again.

C   I tell them sleep deprivation is a form of torture.

B   Again and again.

M   If you commit suicide you'll only have to come back go through it again.

B   The same lesson, again and again.

A   Thou shalt not kill thyself.

C   Vanity, not sanity, will keep me intact.

M   Do you ever hear voices?

B   Only when they talk to me.

A   Weary souls with dry mouths.

C   I'm not ill, I just know that life is not worth living.

A   I've lost my faith in honesty.

B   Lost my faith in

M   Forwards, upwards, onwards,

C   Lost.

B   199714424

M   Move on.

C   I do not trust

M   I do not care

C   Out, out into what?

A   A black fucking hole of half-love.

M   Move on.

A   I hate the consoled and the consoler.

C   I am much fucking angrier than you think.

A   I cannot trust you and I cannot respect you.

C   I am no longer honest.

A   You took that from me and I cannot love you.

M   Back to life.

C   An empty car park which I never can leave.

B   Fear rumbles over the city sky.

M   Absence sleeps between the buildings at night,

C   Between the cars in the lay-by,

B   Between the day and the night.

A   I have to be where I'm meant to be.

B   Let

C   Me

M   Go

A   The outside world is vastly overrated.

   A pause.

C   Let the day perish in which I was born
   Let the blackness of the night terrify it
   Let the stars of its dawn be dark
   May it not see the eyelids of the morning
   Because it did not shut the door of my mother's womb

B   The thing that I fear comes upon me.

C   I hate you,

B   I need you,

M   Need more,

C Need change.

A All the totally predictable and sickening futility that is our relationship.

M I want a real life,

B A real love,

A One that is rooted and grows upwards in daylight.

C What's she got that I haven't got?

A Me.

B The things I want, I want with you.

M It's just. Not. Me.

A There are no secrets.

M There is only blindness.

A You've fallen in love with someone that doesn't exist.

C No.

M Yes.

B No.

A Yes.

C No.

B No.

M Yes.

C I knew this,

B I knew this,

C Why can't I learn?

A I won't settle for a life in the dark.

B Don't look at the sun, don't look at the sun.

C I love you.

M Too late.

A It's over.

C (*Emits a formless cry of despair.*)

   A silence.

A We don't know we're born.

C What have they done to me? What have they done to
   me? What have they done to me? What have they done
   to me? What have they done to me? What have they
   done to me? What have they done to me? What have
   they done to me? What have they done to me? What
   have they done to me? What have they done to me?
   What have they done to me? What have they done to
   me? What have they done to me? What have they done
   to me? What have they done to me? What have they
   done to me?

M Grow up and stop blaming mother.

A Life happens.

B Like flowers,

C Like sunshine,

A Like nightfall.

C A motion away,

B Not a motion towards.

A It is not my fault.

C As if the direction makes any difference.

M Nobody knows.

B My heart is broken.

A It was never my fault.

M You kept coming back.

B Now and forever.

A I am not fighting for you any more.

B   The vision.

M   The loss.

C   The pain.

A   The loss.

B   The gain.

M   The loss.

C   The light.

B   If you died it would be like my bones had been removed.
No one would know why, but I would collapse.

C   If I could be free of you,

B   If I could be free,

M   No that's not it,

A   No not at all,

B   That is not what I meant at all.

A   I broke her heart, what more do I want?

C   The vision.

M   The light.

C   The pain.

A   The light.

M   The gain.

B   The light.

C   The loss.

B   A circle is the only geometric shape defined by its centre.
No chicken and egg about it, the centre came first, the
circumference follows. The earth, by definition, has a
centre. And only the fool that knows it can go wherever
he pleases, knowing the centre will hold him down, stop
him flying out of orbit. But when your sense of centre

shifts, comes whizzing to the surface, the balance has gone. The balance has gone. The balance my baby has gone.

C When she left –

B The spine of my life is broken.

A Why is light given to one in misery

C Bring her back.

A And life to the bitter in soul

B If you were here –

M I am here.

A Like a deep summer shadow.

C I love her I miss her

B I'm through.

M Move on.

C Why did I not die at birth

M Come forth from the womb

B And expire

A Move in shadows, once in a fog.

M Pain is a shadow.

A The shadow of my lie.

C Red rock of ages

B You're not a bad person, you just think too much.

C Let me hide myself.

M Can you

C Would you

B Will you

M Move on.

A Never again I swear to Christ.

B If I lose my voice I'm through.

M Still here.

B But I won't,

C Not this time,

B Not me.

C Not yet.

M It's like waiting for your hair to grow.

B Estás astravesada como el día Miércoles.

C That's me. Exist in the swing. Never still, never one thing or the other, always moving from one extreme to the furthest reaches of the other.

B Sweet.

A One touch.

B So fucking sweet.

M Record.

C Where's my personality gone?

A I'm too old for this.

M Couldn't love you less.

B Couldn't love you more.

M To be perfectly honest,

C (when am I ever 'perfectly honest'?)

B Take no more.

A beat.

C This never happened.

A silence.

A   What I sometimes mistake for ecstasy is simply the absence of grief.

M   Fear nothing.

B   All or nothing.

C   None of it,

B   All of it,

M   None.

C   I am an emotional plagiarist, stealing other people's pain, subsuming it into my own until

A   I can't remember

B   Whose

C   Any more

A   Maybe you're all right,

C   Maybe I'm bad,

A   But God has blessed me with the mark of Cain.

C   Weight.

B   Don't know.

M   Date.

A   Don't know.

B   Fate.

C   Don't know.

A   It's a punishment for hedging your bets.

M   Keep coming back.

B   Again and again.

A   The eternal return.

B   If I lose my voice I'm fucked.

C   Shit on a plate. Look enthusiastic or your own mother will take you apart.

M Get the Night Men in.

A My life is nothing special,

C A stream of haphazard events like any other,

A A stream into a salty ocean that stings, it stings, but does not kill.

M You're dead to me.

B An act of love.

C You're not my mother.

A We were many things.

B Something clicked.

M But I would never say that we were ever in love.

B Found her

A Loved her

C Lost her

M End.

  A silence.

C Something has lifted,

A Outside the city,

B Before the shit started,

A Above the city,

C Another dream,

M I crossed a river that runs in shadow,

B In den Bergen, da fühlst du dich frei,

M One wish,

C A cool summer and a mild winter,

B No fights, no floods,

C   Darkness surrounds a collapsing star,

A   A long deep sleep with you in my arms,

B   No one nothing no shit,

C   Assimilated but not obliterated,

A   Peace,

M   A sickly glare with no single source,

A   A pale gold sea under a pale pink sky,

M   A distant bell crosses the empty sea,

B   Clouds converge as I see I am on a globe,

C   Waves sob like a pulse.

   A beat.

B   Here I am, once again, here I am, here I am, in the darkness, once again,

A   On the edge of nothing,

B   Here I am,

C   Hold my hand,

A   Glory be to the Father,

M   The truth is behind you,

B   I'd give it all up for you,

C   Into the light,

A   As it was in the beginning,

C   Beyond the darkness,

M   And ever shall be,

B   Into the light,

A   At the end of the day it comes back to this,

B   Gaining time,

A   It comes back to me,

M   But losing light,

A   It comes back to this,

C   Fat and shiny and dead dead dead serene,

M   I can't save you,

A   And clean.

C   Other lives

B   No fucker can.

M   Rolled into a ball.

A   Deliver my soul from the sword.

B   I wake as I dream,

M   Alone.

A   Which passeth all understanding.

C   I don't dream any more,

A   I have no dreams.

B   Gaining light,

C   I crossed a river,

M   But losing time.

B   I can't say no to you.

C   To be free of memory,

M   Free of desire,

C   Lie low, provoke nothing,

B   Say nothing.

A   Invisible.

C   When even dreams aren't private

B   Best to forget.

A   Random acts of meaningless joy.

M   You made love by the river.

All   Forget.

A beat.

B   Rape me.

A pause.

M   Is it possible?

C   Cured my body can't cure my soul.

A   I am so tired.

B   I keep coming back.

M   Be the one.

C   Patch and paint and paste a look onto my face.

B   My life in black and white in reverse.

M   Complete.

A   Do what thou wilt shall be the whole of the law.

M   Now.

A   Love is the law, love under will.

C   I feel nothing, nothing.
      I feel nothing.

A   Satan, my lord, I am yours.

B   *(Quietly, continuously, until the end of* **A***'s speech.)*
      no no no no no no no/no no no no no no no no no

A   And don't forget that poetry is language for its own sake.
      Don't forget when different words are sanctioned, other
      attitudes required.
      Don't forget decorum.
      Don't forget decorum.

A beat.

B　Kill me.

　　A beat.

A　Free-falling

B　Into the light

C　Bright white light

A　World without end

C　You're dead to me

M　Glorious. Glorious.

B　And ever shall be

A　Happy

B　So happy

C　Happy and free.

Notes

Page 8   *El dinero viene solo.* (Spanish)
          'Money comes alone.'

Page 15   *Meni ni iz džepa, ni u džep.* (Serbo-Croatian)
          'It's neither in my pocket nor out of it.'

Page 20   *Du bist die Liebe meines Lebens.* (German)
          'You are the love of my life.'

Page 24   *Besos brujos que me matan.* (Spanish)
          'Witches' kisses that kill me.'

Page 27   *Jebem radoznale.* (Serbo-Croatian)
          'I'm fucking the curious.'

Page 42   *Estás astravesada como el día Miércoles.* (Spanish)
          'You are like a Wednesday.'

Page 44   *In den Bergen, da fühlst du dich frei.* (German)
          'In the mountains, there you feel free.'

KING ALFRED'S COLLEGE
LIBRARY

also available

Blasted
Phaedra's Love
Cleansed
4.48 Psychosis
Complete Plays